www.finishinglinepress.com

Afterglow

poems by

Adrian Schnall

Finishing Line Press
Georgetown, Kentucky

Afterglow

ACKNOWLEDGMENTS

My thanks to the editors of the following publications, where the poems
noted below first appeared, some of them in a different form:

JAMA: "Dona Nobis Pacem," "Memorial Day"
The Cuyahoga County Public Library Website: "Fields"
Mizmor Anthology: "Mother Wouldn't Listen to Wagner"
The Cleveland Plain Dealer/cleveland.com: "Granddad Loneliness"
Amethyst Review: "Ice Age"
Pathogens and Immunity: "Celebrity," "Flu Shot," "Death Certificate," "Time,"
"Bittersweet"

Publisher: Leah Huete de Maines
Editor: Christen Kincaid
Cover Art: Sunny K. Kohn
Author Photo: Andrea Schnall
Cover Design: Elizabeth Maines McCleavy

Order online: www.finishinglinepress.com
also available on amazon.com

Author inquiries and mail orders:
Finishing Line Press
PO Box 1626
Georgetown, Kentucky 40324
USA

Contents

I.

Conversation

What to say
when she hasn't uttered a human
sound for months, except the grunts
you've tried to turn into words.

What to say
at 2 AM when the ER doc's
first question is, *Are you the son
with the Power of Attorney?*

Her face a portrait of tranquility,
lips and eyelids pursed symmetrically,
hovering at the edge of absolute peace.
You will your own mouth to move, speak loud

in her left ear, the good one, though
not good at all with no aid in,
*Mother it's me. Can you hear?
Do you know who I am?*

Silence. You start to draw away,
ashamed. When through the harmony
of beeps a single syllable sounds—
a couldn't-be-clearer *Yes.*

You feel your color rise, you haven't tried
to hold her hand. Under the covers you find
a motionless damp rag, you squeeze—
not the slightest stirring in reply.

Your fingers speak, you can only pray
she understands. Her face is stone,
lids placid, nostrils with oxygen prongs,
mouth as though it has never spoken.

A minute by the clock, your tongue
breaks loose. *Mother, are you okay?*
And clear as before, all matter of fact,
those marble lips say, *No.*

Dona Nobis Pacem

Mother is talking to a stranger in the waiting room
when I rush in. *He was telling me the pain
wasn't bad*, she says, *then he went quiet.*
They're old friends now. She and Mrs. Taub

have spent half an hour reliving their parents'
childhoods in Galicia. She looks my way—
A blessing to have someone here, she says,
I don't think I could do this alone.

Silence is not peace. Peace is listening
to the Agnus Dei of a Palestrina mass.

Two white coats at the door—you know
the news is bad when they come in pairs.
They lead me to where he lies, a room
bare of implements of healing.

Every sign of struggle erased. I hesitate,
bend down, touch the white face with my lips.
It's what one does. I am not prepared
for coldness. I do not expect caverns for eyes.

Emptiness is not peace. Peace is gently
shifting chords, endless harmonies.

I wish I had touched him more
like that, before.

Fields

We used to call them particles,
now the experts say there's no such thing.
That electron I thought the tiniest
piece of the universe an imposter,
a shadow—a corner of a fold in a field
that runs through everything.

I know how that electron feels
when I walk into a voting booth,
when I log in at the monitor
where my dentist's receptionist used to be,
when I'm part of The Wave
at Progressive Field.

I know how it feels
as I look beyond the rows of stones,
still and straight in perfect lines
like soldiers readying for a parade,
and see what's left of the field
that has spread out here for centuries—
a billion separate blades of grass,
and all I see a sea of green.

The stone I've come for has a name,
my grandma Ida's, one so different
from all the rest, and yet the same.

No particles in memory,
just fields—of energy, of spirits.
Some smile, some laugh, some smirk,
some wave their arms.
They look and sound the same
as the last time they touched me.

Some day before long will find
no one left who knew Ida's smile,
heard her weep. Rain and wind
will wear the stone smooth
and anyone who looks
will see a nameless speck
in a great green field.

Celebrity

I met you one time,
Johnny Cash.
I was the one in the robin's egg blue mask
threading a line
to the left anterior descending
of your heart.

Your drummer told us how
your chest was caught in a giant vise,
van hurtling down an Interstate,
how that booming baritone
of yours could barely croak out
"hospital."

Did you hear
every mask and gown in the room
let out a cheer
when the plugged-up pipe
deep in your chest
flowed free?

That wasn't applause
for a top ten vocalist,
nor for the hand
that coiled the snake so expertly.
No, that was a cheer for life!

You sent us each a country ham.
Other days we weren't so lucky.

Splinter

"Do what you need to," I said.

As though this were extracting
an arrowhead buried in flesh,
not a sliver of wood from a pinky.

She my officemate, colleague,
friend. But not—
it occurred to me as she started
to probe—a surgeon.
Probably hadn't fingered
a forceps in years.

What I warn my patients
against every day—
not wise to compromise
with convenience.

I had no fear of pain.
A dozen tours in the OR,
years of drawing blood—
we learn to distance,
numb ourselves.

Numb ourselves, that is,
to the pain of another—
my pinky should have taken
itself to Urgent Care.

Maybe there was hurt,
but I never noticed.
All I recall is a flood
of sweetness, a drowsy
warmth, as when the world
is about to go dark.

Sometimes as we're falling
we hear a voice calling
in the distance.

"Oh, shit—going vagal,"
this one said.

It sounded like mine.

Flu Shot

Hold it like a dart,
squeeze the skin,
use your wrist.
She'll feel nothing
but that gentle
twist.

She looks away.
"Shall I tell you when"? I say,
smiling as I drop the used syringe
in the sharp-safe bin.
I live for that look
of disbelief.

I do not speak to her
of the debacle of '76.
Swine flu panic in the air,
half the population
clamoring for the needle.
In the aftermath,
two hundred with Guillain-Barré,
thirty dead.
It was worth it, the experts said.
We saved millions from the flu.

Not worth it for Jonathan,
who lived the worst ten days of his life
on life support in ICU,
nerve fibers eaten away,
ravaged by that malady.
He couldn't talk for a week,
took a month to walk,
a twenty-five-year-old
with an old man's limp.

He never got the shot again,
didn't need to read the headlines.

No black plague descended in '76,
no swine flu, even in those
who chose not to get stuck.

Yet I still immunize,
proselytize for it.

I watch Jonathan
limp across the room
and try to remember:
millions have been saved
in other years.

Granddad Loneliness

He has his father's smile,
and tells me with a twinkle
his dad is being almost good
at social distancing.
Facetime—amazing!

On the screen he shows me
the prints on his walls, the view
from his window. He's smart
and silly and wonderful,
and suddenly says *I love you.*
A smile is etched on my face
for the next hour.

Who knew two weeks is all it takes
for the world to turn to stone?
Round-the-clock pandemic news,
stacks of Great Books, vintage CD's,
three seasons of Law and Order—
you don't need to wait for the ending,
they're all the same story.

Calls to check on children,
siblings, nieces, nephews,
every friend I have alive,
each trying to walk a line
between stupid and paranoid.
So far everyone fine,
no one not afraid.

On CNN I see the clip
of a woman weeping
outside a nursing home,
mouthing to her mom
through a pane of glass—
my Facetime chat

was so much better,
yet in an eerie way
the same.

II.

Death Certificate

How far back in the chain to go?
I'm penning in an entry
on the parchment of public record,
creating a statistic for the students of disease,
but writing too the final word
on the last page of the book
for the bereaved.

So robust, barrel of a woman,
layered in corsets from another century.
Her heart went dead December first,
but Staphylococci started
seeding her veins three days before,
breeding in the purple sore
that showed its color Labor Day.
An ulcer on her bottom,
branded there by months of sitting
staring at air. We lost her when
her mind burned out in May.

Should I say dementia killed her?
Not enough space
for a dissertation
on causation and its subtleties.
I can't just call it stoppage
of the clock—
that's one frame
out of thousands
in a documentary.
I settle for "Septicemia, Staph."
The statisticians will be pleased,
two different categories.

And there's her daughter's face,
and grandchildren at peace,
remembering her as maimed
by an invading legion,
forgetting
her forgetting
of their names.

Time

My index finger was reaching for
the up button on the elevator
when the voice sounded above,
Code Blue Tower 8. Code Blue Tower 8.
I broke for the stairs.

They were getting the paddles in place;
the First Year with the floppy hair, Ethan,
pumping the chest; the Night Float,
Emily, manning an Ambu-Bag;
Jamie, the Resident, running the code.

I dared a look at the face—
Ken, with whom I'd traded jokes
for twenty years—Ken, whom I'd told
yesterday his time was coming—
he'd be back home, maybe two days.

Clear! barked Jamie. Hands backed away,
motion suspended. A very long second.
The shape on the bed gave a shudder.
Then Jamie's voice: *Excellent, a rhythm.*

A rhythm—but no pulse.
Hands were pumping again,
counting, squeezing in air.
The spark was there on the screen—
life, dancing across it—
but none of the tiny muscles
in the heart were listening.

Epi. Atropine. Thirty minutes.
Ethan looked up at Jamie, she
shot a glance at me. Someone
had to say it—and first
right of refusal to the guy
with gray hair.

A power none of us wished for—
a power none of us have—
but the world pretends.

I felt my head move up and down.
Jamie's eyes found the clock—
7:44 AM, she said. *Time.*

Memorial Day

I hold it, feel its weight—
a paper chart, a relic.
She died six months before
we went electronic.

Memento of a face,
of cookies, chocolate cake;
of bonds we form,
mistakes we make.

This day each year I walk
down rows of stones,
speak names, hear laughter,
see shapes, smiles, frowns—

and bring this sheaf of
a life back out into light.
To take it home was wrong,
though the space between wrong and right

seems to shrink as I look back.
It should have been marked in red,
"Expired," stored on a shelf,
labeled with a date to be fed

to a shredder. Instead, I secreted
it to my own dark place.
It wasn't the only file
I'd wanted to keep, to face

from time to time. Something
there is in a presence—an urn,
a stone, a thing of substance—
that helps us to return

to the sorrow, to accept it
or not, to re-live the dying—
to explain, or beg forgiveness—
to move past it, or keep trying.

Ice Age

A new kind of climate change—
trees alive with birdsong,
but a feeling of lead in the air.
A sky that should dazzle the eye—
but a veil of mist even there.

A poet once said the lost
are like this—frozen
in spirit, caught in ice.
How to break free,
get to live twice?

I tell myself the birds
came back long ago from the frost.
Somehow they managed to nest,
even on glaciers. I love the thought
of them snuggling, breast

to breast, wing to wing.
It's how one survives
an age like this—
how one keeps alive
the fire to sing.

Winter Solstice

Frozen fountains, granite earth—
we've spun to the end of our string,
worlds away from light.

Juices in need of transfusion
gone deep, seeking roots,
hungry to be born.

The eye must be used to the dark
to behold the birthing,
the glow before

the glimmer, the blush before
the peacock spread
of wings.

We must live a time in silence
before we can hear
cries in the trees.

On the road to the shore
one can taste salt air
miles from the sea.

Evanescence

No breeze along the lake
but the chill and the morning slant
of light make ghosts of branches.
My mind re-leaves bare limbs,
fills out the shape of trees,
but the sky sees only skeletons,
or veins, or arteries.

And a single maple leaf—
brilliant, supple, alive—
floats at the edge of sight,
drifting down but swaying,
rocking left and right.

I want to sing that lonely thing
to sleep. I wish you were here
touching my hand, sharing
a smile, remembering
an infant who refused to rest
until rocked to the strains
not of a lullaby, but of
Home on the Range.

Before I can blurt out
a note or a word
the flight is done.
The moment,
the lightness,
gone.

Summer Solstice

Feasts and celebrations—
brightness and warmth
forever, no end!

How can so many
be suckered by earthly
tilt, by one day's spin?

A dozen languages,
scores of cultures,
tell the same lie.

We exult in the sun,
with half our planet
floundering in night.

While blazes we've ignited
rage on, consuming,
breeding no light.

As we spin at the end of a string
around a swirling mass
of mindless atoms

that crash, explode, fuse,
transmute into sparks—
today's dumb glow—

and oblivious we dance
and sing hosannas to Apollo,
blinded by sight.

III.

Veterans Day

Shot down in a jungle,
eight thousand miles away—
me not at his side.

I never knew how or at
what hour. All I had left
was a hollow, a hope
that it happened quick,
that he didn't die abandoned.
Did his widow ask?
Would any answer have made
the gash less deep?

Blind luck—some Chicken Colonel
found reason to call up the 184th.
A different flick of his wrist,
the pin on his board would have been
the 183rd. The me I was then
would have saluted—to be young
is to be stupid—and the widow
would have been mine.

I never saw The Wall
'til twenty years later—fifty-eight
thousand chiseled names.
My eyes stuck on a woman's
fingers—lingering—tracing
letters left to right,
spelling out a life.

On the news today a soldier
was interviewed next to The Wall.
"At least these guys didn't die
for nothing," he said.

And I wondered how "for nothing"
is spelled in Pashto. In Arabic.
In Vietnamese. In French,
German, Russian, Japanese.
How they said it long ago
in Troy, in Greece.

Bittersweet

The winner has been declared.
A flood of relief!
Exultation!
Dancing in the streets!

And a gasp of horror.
How can there be tens of millions
on the other side? So many more
than a couple dozen Proud Boys,
a few towns of hillbilly farmers,
a frenzied rally crowd
chanting *Lock her up.*

It's fathers and mothers,
sisters and brothers.
Is it them or us?
Who are the blind?

Fires still flare on the battlefield—
one rages on in the distance.
But every blaze is dying as I watch,
great conflagrations
turning to ash.

The forecast is for snow
on the mountaintops, in the streets,
in the corridors of State.

I think the air will be clear
in the morning. I think I will hear
music in the trees.

But no one is surrendering
his gun.

Florida Man Announces Candidacy

Light leaches from the sky
in a six-block trip to the market.
Gusts rock my Prius. A red
Ford pickup swears, honks
furiously. Pellets of rain take
aim at me in the parking lot.

Two years ago, same drive,
same downpour, my grocery
list on a page of The Times.
How could I not see the headline?
"He calls fallen soldiers *losers*"—
with a shot of Mr. Trump
among gravestones.

We lost so many that year!
The noble whose time had come—
John Lewis, RBG, Toni Morrison.
Lives lost to hate, millions
to pestilence. Of my own,
a precious sister, two cousins,
a beloved friend.

Me battered by sheets of rain
and grief. Now a gale again—
sirens, disaster warnings—
echoes of the living lost,
a world where consolation
and kindness are quarantined.

I'm waterlogged, drenched
in darkness—but can't
not battle the storm.
I'll replenish blueberries,
bananas. Bring home
a quart of milk. And a loaf
of bread.

Trial

Six wounded, eleven dead—
and he could have stormed

any synagogue, any
city. Now his life

dangling—turning not
on blindness dressed

in a bullet-proof vest,
but on the lens

of sight. Is a soul
sitting there?

Or an embodiment?
Will the posse stare

through his chair without
seeing? Or will one

in twelve hear the
shrieks in his head?

There can be no forgiveness,
cries a voice

in the gallery—
echo of a usurer

in an ancient play.
Black imaginings—

if only we could all
be sequestered.

A sentence will
be pronounced

on everyone
in the room.

IV.

Mother Wouldn't Listen to Wagner

I'd listened a dozen times.
How could I never have heard the hate before?
Mussorgsky's "Pictures at an Exhibition,"
where he writes about the Jews.
Schmuyle with the high-pitched wheedling voice.
Goldenberg the banker, icicles for fingers.

I loved the ugliness in those faces,
loved the ugly oxcart
rumbling on wooden wheels,
loved his ugly Baba Yaga,
the child-devouring witch.
Then I read his letters:
obbligato loathing and contempt.

Yet how he could paint those perfect
attitudes! How he could make them
breathe and speak with nothing
but pitch and key and beat!
The beauty is still there for me,
just not as warm to touch.
I'll listen to "Pictures" again.

Mother would not approve.
She'd stiffen at the mention of Wagner's name.
No Lohengrin in her house.
She'd look as though about to spit.
He called us animals.
He should burn in Hell!
For me he doesn't exist!

I cannot find it in myself
to carry the burden of spite that far.

Would I feel different if, like her,
I'd heard my father's first-hand memories
of cousins and Polish schoolyard friends
slaughtered in village massacres?
If, like her, I'd heard the radio in '45
blaring out horrors of Auschwitz and Buchenwald
and wept at the thought that that's
why Uncle Paul did not write back?

Whenever I listen to Lohengrin
I see that look in mother's eye
and wonder if somewhere she's looking down,
thinking I've betrayed our blood.
Then I listen a little longer
to the glowing harmonies
and feel a flood of sadness
for all the eyes blinded by hate,
and wonder what it takes
to wring out a drop
of forgiveness.

Generosity

All I've got is eleven bucks
and change, you say;
and you watch the razor
trembling at your throat,
hear the desperation
in his mumbling.

No time to worry he
might grab your ID,
or the bookbag with
your term-paper on Stalin.

You wait for the blade to slice,
picture the crimson trail,
but he's scrambling
down College Street,
your fingers at your neck—
is it still whole?

You wish you'd had more to give—
he had nowhere else to go,
he could barely speak
for the shaking.
And how much would you
have paid for the privilege
of waking up
one more day?

You hand that paper in
on Stalin having his inner
circle shot, one by one.

You tell the police
you never saw
the guy's face.

Date Night

Was it "Chic of Araby,"
the sundae you had
that night at Boukair's?

Was it "Pillow Talk"
or "That Touch of Mink"
we saw?

They're all gone now,
Doris, Cary, Rock—
gone the way

Boukair's is gone,
like the Halle Brothers
and Sterling Lindner

windows we walked
by. Surely those
American Legion

guys are gone,
the ones who circled
round us simpering,

weaving unseen
thread to pull
two teenagers

together, closer
than we dared
to come ourselves.

Some things one never
forgets—dazzle
of lights, scoop

upon scoop
of sweetness,
sizzle between

Doris and Rock—
and those silly men
in their red flight caps.

Our secret—like
the bed fashioned
from a living tree

in the Odyssey.
Like what a stranger
told us yesterday

as we floated down
Euclid Avenue
again, hand in hand—

two youngsters
fifty years later.
How he stopped

and smirked
and told us
Get a room.

Funeral Oration

The rabbi is doing his best
to squeeze light out of darkness,
make us forget what lies ahead
by looking back.

And a tiny bundle in swaddling
in the middle of the second row
belts out a torrent of screams.
My soul is restored.

Grating and raging and beautiful,
a creature announcing its animal
existence, nothing else matters.

The mother cradles, caresses
but soon is fleeing up the aisle
in a crescendo of wails.

Joy mixed with grief,
but the mother can't see it.
A strange arithmetic—
plus one added to minus one
equals two.

Pieces remain,
remembrances
of the thing that's been lost.

One part recedes,
another part grows.
The little one knows—
nothing else matters.

Making Music

Thetis held him by the heel
to dip him, steel his skin.
Don't all mothers
do the same?

Each of us armor safe
from spears and arrows,
armored too from touch,
from other voices,
from the sounding
of our own.

Each of us muffled,
mummified,
left to thrust
with elbows
and knees,
struggle alone.

Only the few
break through,
defy the curse—

breathe deep,
play sweet,
sing loud.

In Appreciation

To the lecturers and workshop leaders at the Bread Loaf Writer's Conference—in particular Eavan Boland, A. E. Stallings, Ilya Kaminski and Sally Keith—I will be forever grateful for your generosity, inspiration and wisdom.

To the poets in the Butcher Shop, a huge thank you for your laughter, sophistication, and friendly chopping up of my poems month after month.

To Bill Newby, my good friend and colleague in literature, poetry and life, thanks for your generous support and sharing.

To David Swerdlow, to whom I will always be profoundly grateful for friendship, poetic insights, and sage advice, and without whom this book would never have come together.

Above all, eternal thanks to my wife Andrea, my first and still first reader, who made me feel I could do this; and without whose love, support, and poetic ear not one of these poems would ever have seen the light.